I Wonder Why

Pyramids Were Built

and Other Questions About Ancient Egypt

Philip Steele

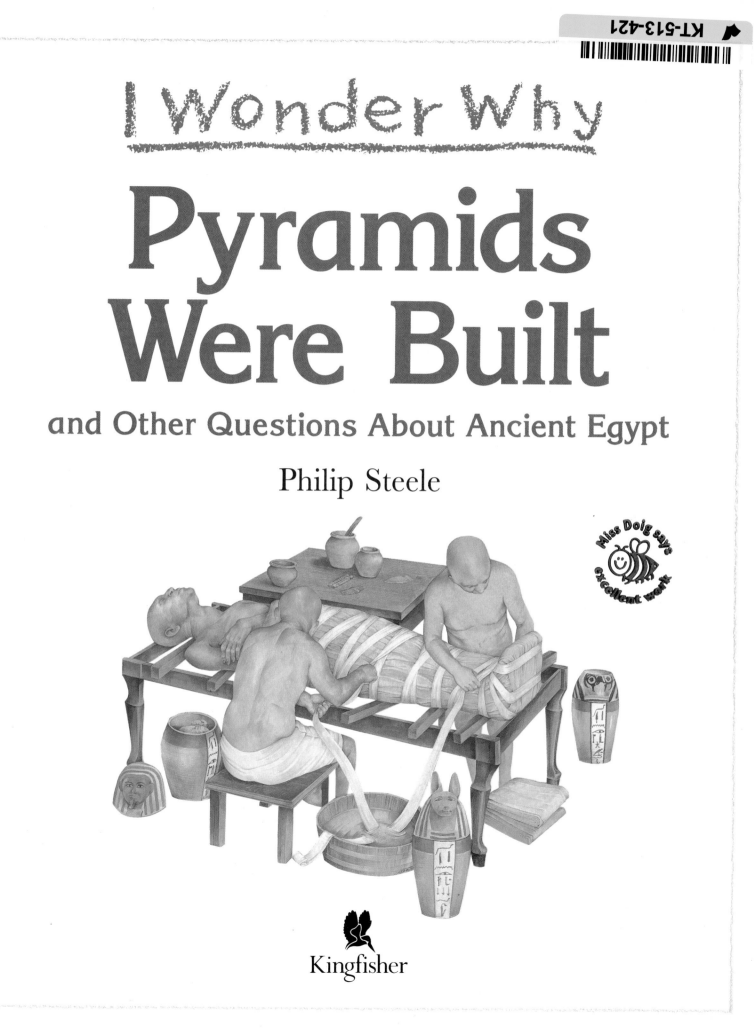

Kingfisher

KINGFISHER
An imprint of Larousse plc
Elsley House, 24-30 Great Titchfield Street,
London, W1P 7AD

First published by Kingfisher 1995
(hb) 10 9 8 7 6 5 4 3 2 1
(pb) 10 9 8 7 6 5 4 3 2 1
Copyright © Larousse plc 1995

A CIP catalogue record for this book is available from
the British Library

ISBN 1 85697 296 8 (hb)
     1 85697 312 3 (pb)

Phototypeset by Tradespools Ltd, Frome, Somerset
Printed and bound in Italy

Series editor: Jackie Gaff
Series designer: David West Children's Books
Author: Philip Steele
Consultant: Department of Egyptian Antiquities,
    British Museum
Editors: Claire Llewellyn, Clare Oliver
Art editor: Christina Fraser
Cover illustrations: Chris Forsey, cartoons by
    Tony Kenyon (B.L. Kearley)
Illustrations: Peter Dennis (Linda Rogers Associates)
    14-15, 24-25, 28-29; Chris Forsey 12-13;
    Luigi Galante (Virgil Pomfret Agency) 4-5, 16-17;
    Nick Harris (Virgil Pomfret Agency) 18-19, 22-23;
    Adam Hook (Linden Artists) 8-9, 26-27, 30-31;
    Tony Kenyon (B.L. Kearley) all cartoons;
    Nicki Palin 6-7, 10-11, 20-21.

CONTENTS

Why do we call Egyptians ancient?

We call the Egyptians ancient because they lived such a long time ago – not because they all reached a ripe old age! The first Egyptians were farmers about 8,000 years ago. Within a few thousand years, Egypt had become one of the most powerful countries in the world.

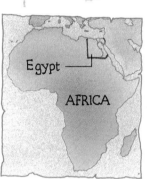

Egypt
AFRICA

● Will people be studying us in 5,000 years' time? What will they think about the way we live now?

● The Egyptians usually built tombs for dead kings on the river's western bank, where the Sun sets. They believed that their kings went to meet the Sun god when they died.

● Egypt is mostly sandy desert, where nothing grows. The Ancient Egyptians settled on the banks of the river Nile, where there was plenty of water for themselves and their crops.

● The Ancient Egyptians didn't know about distant parts of the world. But they did explore parts of Asia and Africa. And their merchants bought wood, gold, ivory, spices and even apes from nearby countries.

Why were the Egyptians great?

The Egyptians were so good at farming that they became very rich. They built fantastic temples for their gods, and huge pointed tombs called pyramids where they buried their kings. They had armies and ships and courts of law. Their priests studied the stars and their craftspeople made beautiful things from gold and silver.

Mediterranean Sea

Giza
Memphis
Saqqara

LOWER EGYPT

Red Sea

Abydos
Valley of the Kings
Thebes

UPPER EGYPT

Nile River

Farming land
Desert

Who ruled Egypt?

The king of Egypt was called the pharaoh. The Egyptians believed that their Sun god Re was the first king of Egypt, and that all the pharaohs after him were his relatives. This made the pharaoh very holy – and very powerful! The people thought he was a god on Earth.

● The pharaoh's advisors were called the Honoured Ones. There were all sorts of royal officials, too, with grand names like the Director of Royal Dress and the Keeper of the Royal Wigs.

Could a woman be pharaoh?

Although very few women ruled Egypt, there was a famous pharaoh called Hatshepsut. When her six-year-old nephew came to the throne, Hatshepsut was asked to rule Egypt for him – just until he was a little bit older. But Hatshepsut liked ruling so much that she wouldn't let her nephew take over. He didn't get the chance to rule until he was 30 years old!

● When she was pharaoh, Hatshepsut had to wear the badges of royalty. These included a false beard, made of real hair.

How would you know if you met a pharaoh?

He would be wearing a crown, of course! In fact, pharaohs sometimes wore two crowns at the same time – a white one for Upper Egypt, which was the name for the south of the country, and a red one for Lower Egypt, which was the north.

Who was the crocodile god?

In old paintings and carvings, most Egyptian gods and goddesses have animal heads. The water god, Sebek, was shown as a crocodile. Thoth had the head of a bird called an ibis, while Taweret looked like a hippo! Osiris and Isis were luckier. They were shown as a great king and queen.

● The Egyptians loved to wear lucky charms. Their favourites were scarabs. The scarab beetle was sacred to the Sun god, Re.

● The Ancient Egyptians worshipped as many as 2,000 gods and goddesses!

Thoth, god of learning

Osiris, god of death

Who was the goddess Nut?

Nut was goddess of the heavens and she was usually shown covered in stars. Many gods and goddesses were linked in families. Nut was married to Geb. Isis and Osiris were their children.

● Being a priest was a part-time job. Most only spent 3 months a year at the temple, and lived at home the rest of the time.

BACK IN 9 MONTHS

● Priests had to wash twice during the day and twice at night, to make themselves clean and pure for the gods.

Taweret, goddess of childbirth and babies

Isis, wife of Osiris

Why did the Egyptians bury their mummies?

A mummy is a dead body which has been dried out so it lasts for thousands of years. The Egyptians believed that the dead travelled to another world, where they needed their bodies. And they didn't want any bits missing!

- Some poorer families had their nearest and dearest mummified, but it was an expensive business. Only the rich could afford a really good send-off.

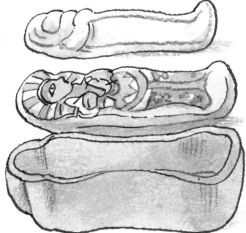

- The mummy was placed inside a series of wooden coffins. These were put in a big stone case called a sarcophagus.

- Monkeys, crocodiles, cats and other sacred animals were often mummified, too!

Why were mummies brainless?

The Ancient Egyptians believed that the heart was the most important part of the whole body. They thought that the brain was useless. So when they were preparing a mummy, they took out the brain – by pulling it down through the nose!

Why were mummies wrapped in bandages?

Wrapping the dead body helped to keep its shape. After the insides were removed, the body was dried out for 40 days in salty stuff called natron. Then it was washed, rubbed with ointments, and tightly bandaged.

Why were the pyramids built?

The pyramids were huge tombs for dead pharaohs and other very important people. No one knows exactly why the pyramids were shaped this way. Some people think they were built to point towards the Sun and stars, so that the dead person's spirit could fly to heaven like a rocket.

• The Great Pyramid at Giza was built more than 4,500 years ago. This is what it looks like today.

• Pharaohs were buried with all their finest clothes and jewellery, so tombs were given sneaky traps to catch out robbers.

• There are other, smaller pyramids at Giza, and over 80 at other places in Egypt. Some have stepped sides and bent tops.

● This is what the Great Pyramid looks like inside.

Pharaoh's chamber

Who liked to get knee-deep in mud?

Egyptian farmers loved mud – it has all the water and goodness that plants need to grow well. The most important time in a farmer's year was when the Nile flooded and dumped rich, black mud on the dry fields. A good flood meant a good harvest. A bad one meant people went hungry.

● The only farm land in Egypt is near the river Nile. It used to be called the Black Land, because the mud left by the floods was black. The rocky desert was called the Red Land.

● Priests watched the Moon and stars to work out a calendar of the months. This told them when the floods would come and when to plant crops.

● Juicy grapes and fresh green vegetables were grown in the rich Nile mud. Golden ears of wheat and barley were harvested and stored in granaries.

Which was the fastest way to travel?

The quickest route in Egypt was the river Nile. Egyptian boats were made from river reeds or wood. They were the only way to get from one side of the river to the other – unless you swam and liked crocodiles!

● The big question each year was: "How deep is the flood?" Notched stones were used like giant rulers to measure the rising water. The stones were called nilometers.

● Farmers dug ditches to carry water to their crops when the Nile wasn't in flood. They used a clever machine called a shaduf to lift water out of the river into the ditches.

Why did people sit on the roof?

The roof was just about the best spot in an Egyptian house. It was cooler than indoors, especially under a shady canopy. People liked to sit and talk there, or play board games.

● Egyptian houses had flat roofs. Pointed roofs were invented in rainy lands, to let the water drain away.

● Most houses were made of mud bricks, but stone blocks were used for temples, tombs and palaces.

Who made mud pies?

Bricks were made from river mud. Brick-makers trampled the mud with their bare feet until it was sticky. They added bits of straw and reed to make the mixture firmer. Then they shaped the mud pies into bricks, which dried hard in the Sun.

Who had nightmares?

Some Egyptians must have slept well, but their beds do look very uncomfortable! They were made of wood, with ropes or leather straps instead of springs. And people didn't lie on soft pillows filled with feathers. All they had were wooden headrests!

Who had floury feet?

When Egyptian cooks made bread, they sometimes jumped into a huge bowl on the floor and kneaded the dough with their feet. Let's hope they washed them first!

● Egyptian feet were good at making wine, too. Every last drop of juice was trampled from the grapes.

● The Egyptians baked lots of delicious cakes – ring doughnuts, pyramid-shaped buns, and cakes that looked like crocodiles!

What's the world's stalest bread?

Loaves of bread have been found in Egyptian tombs. No one has tasted them, though. The bread is thousands of years old and as hard as rock!

● Wooden lunch boxes full of meat and fruit were sometimes left in tombs, in case the mummy got hungry in the next world!

● Egyptian bread must have been a bit gritty, even when it was fresh, since many of the mummies' teeth are very worn down.

Who had splendid feasts?

Well, poor people certainly didn't! Pharaohs and rich people held fantastic feasts, where they ate juicy pieces of beef, mutton or goose. The meat was sometimes barbequed, and served with crunchy onions or garlic, as well as spinach, leeks, peas or beans. What was for pudding? Juicy figs, sweet melons or pomegranates.

Who looked really cool?

Egypt is a very hot country, and in ancient times people kept cool by wearing as little as possible. Ordinary workers just wore a simple cloth around their waists. But for the rich, the coolest fashion was graceful clothes made from the finest linen.

● Linen is made from a plant called flax. It's very hard to prepare, but the Egyptians could spin and weave it into lengths of beautifully light and flimsy cloth.

● Acrobats and dancing girls just wore strings of beads!

● Women wore long dresses with shoulder straps. Men wore long kilts that hung in folds. Children often wore nothing at all.

Who liked to sparkle?

Most clothes were plain white, so rich people added colour and sparkle by wearing beautiful jewellery made from gold and colourful precious stones.

● Both men and women wore jewellery.

Sometimes, for a special feast, they wore wide cloth collars decorated with leaves, wildflowers or glass-like beads. Poorer people's jewellery was made from copper and shells.

Why did shoes wear out?

Servants' shoes were woven from reeds which they gathered from the river bank. The shoes didn't last long – particularly when the servants had to keep running around after their rich masters and mistresses!

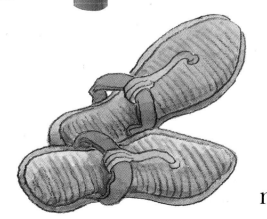

Who loved making up?

Rich Egyptian women wore lots of striking make-up. Eyeshadow went on first, then a black line around the eyes, and finally a rosy lipstick and cheek blusher. The Ancient Egyptians still look beautiful over 4,000 years later – in their paintings!

Why did women wear cones on their heads?

Rich women pinned cones to their wigs for feasts and parties. But they wore cones of perfumed grease, not ice-cream cones! As the greasy cones melted in the warm evening air, they gave off a sweet perfume.

• The Egyptians loved to smell good. Rich people used scented oils and breath fresheners, and they carried sweet-smelling flowers around with them.

• Men liked to look good, so they wore make-up, too.

• The Egyptians took great care of their looks. They mixed up lotions to stop baldness and dandruff — even spots!

Who made a beeline for wigs?

Pharaohs and rich people – everybody who was anybody wore a wig on their head. The wigs were made of real hair, which was tied into hundreds of tiny plaits and held in place by sticky beeswax.

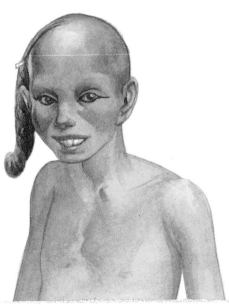

• Young boys' heads were shaved, except for a single plait of hair on the right-hand side.

Who played with lions?

Nobody did, if they had any sense! But young children did play with wooden lions and other toy animals. Children also had spinning tops, as well as balls that rattled, and dolls with beads in their hair.

● Few people could read, so after a day's work they probably sat down to listen to storytellers. There were many exciting tales about gods and goddesses.

● Children ran around playing ball-games or tag, then cooled off with a swim in the river.

Who played board games?

Tutankhamun became pharaoh when he was only 12 years old. He loved playing a board game called senet, and after he died a board was buried with him in his tomb. It is a beautiful set, made of white ivory and a black wood called ebony.

● The senet board had 20 squares on one side and 30 on the other. Experts think it was a bit like ludo.

Did Egyptians like parties?

● Musicians plucked harps, beat drums and tambourines, blew pipes and shook tinkling bells.

The Egyptians might have spent a lot of time building tombs, but they weren't a miserable lot! They loved music and dancing. At rich people's banquets, there were often shows with dancing girls, musicians, acrobats and singers.

25

Why is paper called paper?

Our word 'paper' comes from papyrus, a tall reed that grows beside the Nile. The Egyptians discovered how to use the thready insides of these papyrus reeds to make a kind of paper. It was thicker than the paper we use today, but just as useful.

● Papyrus was expensive because it took so long to make. Quick notes were scribbled on pieces of pottery instead.

1 Paper-makers cut and peeled the reeds.

3 They hammered them until the sticky plant juices glued them together.

4 Next they used a smooth stone or a special tool to rub the surface of the papyrus paper smooth.

2 They cut the reed stems into thin slices and then laid them in rows, one on top of the other.

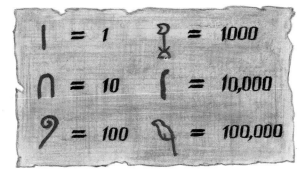

I = 1		⌐ = 1000	
∩ = 10		∫ = 10,000	
ϑ = 100		𝄢 = 100,000	

- There were even pictures for numbers. It can't have been easy doing sums!

- Few children went to school. Some boys trained as scribes, people whose job was writing. They had to learn over 700 hieroglyphs. Spelling tests were a nightmare!

What did Egyptian writing look like?

The first Egyptian writing was made up of rows of pictures, called hieroglyphs. Each picture stood for an object, an idea, or the sound of a word. Many of the hieroglyphs are quite complicated – they must have taken ages to draw!

- The ends of reeds were frayed to make paint-brushes. Ink was made from soot or red earth.

5 Finally, all the pieces of papyrus paper were glued into a long strip and rolled into a scroll.

- These hieroglyphs make up the name CLEOPATRA. Perhaps you can work out how to write TOP CAT or TREACLE.

C L E O P A T R A

Which were the most dangerous animals?

Egypt wasn't always a safe place. Wild bulls and lions lived in the desert, while hungry crocodiles lurked in the river Nile. Many Egyptians enjoyed hunting these animals, even though they could be dangerous.

● Even hippo-hunting could be dangerous. An angry hippo could easily overturn one of the hunter's tiny boats.

● When it died, a pet dog was buried with its collar – all ready for a walk in the after-life!

Did people have pets?

Rich Egyptians had pets, just as we do today, and they loved them just as much. Most people settled for a dog or a cat, but people who really wanted to show off kept pet apes and monkeys.

● Today there are no lions or hippos left in Egypt. They are only found in countries far to the south. But Ancient Egyptians would still recognize birds such as the ibis and the hoopoe.

● The whole family went along on duck hunts. The birds were brought down by sticks, which were a bit like boomerangs – only they didn't come back!

What did Egyptians call their cats?

The Egyptian word for cat was miw – a cross between a mew and a miaow! The Egyptians were probably the first to tame cats. They used them to catch mice in grain stores.

● Ostriches were hunted for their large tail feathers. These were made into beautiful fans to keep rich people cool.

How can you become an Egyptologist?

Egyptologists are people who study Ancient Egypt. To become one, you need to learn all about the history of Egypt, and the things that have survived from that time. Reading books and visiting museums are the best ways to start.

● Howard Carter went to Egypt in 1892, and spent many years excavating Ancient Egyptian tombs. He made his most famous discovery in 1920 – the tomb of the boy-pharaoh Tutankhamun.

● Tutankhamun's mummy was protected by several coffins. The last one was made of solid gold.

Why do mummies have X-rays?

Modern science is a great help to Egyptologists. X-rays can show whether a mummy died from an illness or an accident. They can even tell whether it suffered from toothache!

● Egyptologists can even run tests on the things they find in a mummy's tummy, and work out what its last meal was before it died!

Where can you come face to face with a pharaoh?

Egypt's largest museum is in the capital city of Cairo. Here, you can gaze on the 4,000-year-old faces of the mummified pharaohs. Not all the pharaohs are here, though. Some are still lying peacefully, hidden in their desert tombs.

Index

EGYPTIAN
MUMMIES

Published in Great Britain in 2002
by Book House, an imprint of
The Salariya Book Company Ltd
25 Marlborough Place, Brighton BN1 1UB

Visit the Salariya Book Company at:
www.salariya.com
www.book-house.co.uk

ISBN 1 904194 09 5

A catalogue record for this book is available from the British Library.

Printed and bound in China.

Printed on paper from sustainable forests.

Author:

Henrietta McCall studied

Egyptology at Oxford University. She is the author of **Pyramids** in the *Fast Forward* series and **Mesopotamian Myths**. Henrietta has also edited numerous children's books on ancient Egypt and is a member of the Council of the British Museum Society.

Artist:

Dave Antram was born in Brighton in

1958. He studied at Eastbourne College of Art and then worked in advertising for 15 years before becoming a full-time artist. He has illustrated many children's non-fiction books.

Series creator:

David Salariya was born in Dundee,

Scotland. In 1989 he established The Salariya Book Company. He has illustrated a wide range of books and has created many new series for publishers in the UK and overseas. He lives in Brighton with his wife, illustrator Shirley Willis, and their son.

Editors:

Karen Barker Smith
Stephanie Cole

Additional artists:

Mark Bergin
John James
Carolyn Scrace

EGYPTIAN MUMMIES

Written by
HENRIETTA McCALL

Illustrated by
DAVE ANTRAM

Created and designed by
DAVID SALARIYA

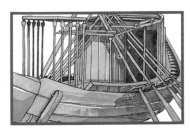

BOOK HOUSE

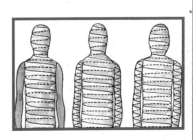

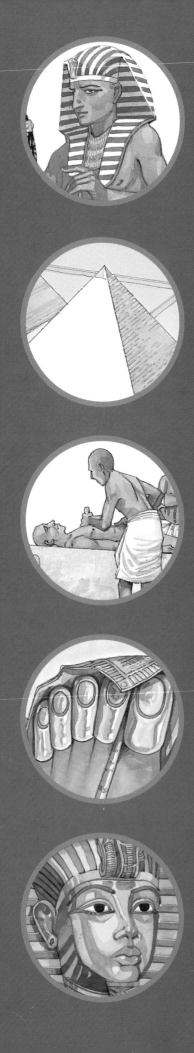

Contents

Ancient Egypt

The ancient land of Egypt was divided into two parts: the Black Land and the Red Land. The Black Land, which the Egyptians called *kemet*, was the fertile land all along the banks of the River Nile. The land was fertile because of the great flood (called the Inundation), which took place every year between July and September. At this time, the river rose higher and higher until it burst its banks and flooded all the nearby countryside with rich, muddy water that turned the land black. Farmers could then sow wheat, barley and vegetables for the coming year. Occasionally, the river did not flood the land, and when this happened many animals and people died of starvation. The Red Land, called *deshret*, consisted of vast areas where nothing would grow. This was where stone was quarried for great temples and tombs and turquoise, malachite and gold were mined.

Shu was the god of light. His son, Geb, was the god of earth, and Shu's daughter, Nut, was goddess of the sky. The ancient Egyptians believed that Nut swallowed the sun at nightfall, that it travelled through her body during the night hours and that at dawn she gave birth to it once more. Nut is often pictured in an arched position, as if she is the sky arched over the flat form of the earth (above).

Each king (also known as a pharaoh) of ancient Egypt usually had many wives, but the most important was called the Chief Royal Wife. She was often the mother of the future king, but may have been the one the king loved the most. The mother of the present king was also an important figure in the royal palace as she had given life to the king.

Chief Royal Wife

Pharaoh

7

Death and Burial

Some people think that the ancient Egyptians were obsessed with death. In fact, the opposite is true. They so much enjoyed their lives in the well-ordered, rich and beautiful land of Egypt that they wanted to live forever. As that was not possible, they wanted their next life, or afterlife, to be just as good as, if not better than, life on earth.

The ancient Egyptians believed that every human had two spiritual parts: the *ba*, which was responsible for a person's character, and the *ka*, which represented a person's life force. When someone died, his *ka* was believed to live on in his physical body, so it was essential to preserve it. This was achieved by a complicated process called mummification.

Only rich people were mummified. Poor people were buried in pits dug in the sand and because Egypt is so dry and hot their bodies were often naturally mummified. The bodily fluids leaked into the hot sand, the body dried out and the skin covering the skeleton became hard and leathery. Objects such as pots or beads were often left beside the body.

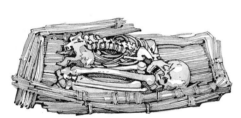

Every Egyptian settlement had its own cemetery, or city of the dead, which Egyptologists call a necropolis. Private citizens were buried there, often with gold jewellery, weapons or finely decorated pottery. Above, a reed coffin.

The low rectangular structure of a mastaba tomb was built of mud brick or stone above an underground chamber. Often the walls of the burial chamber were decorated with scenes of daily life and the dead person was buried with goods for the afterlife.

Step Pyramid   *Bent Pyramid*

Egyptian kings were buried in pyramids. The earliest known pyramid is the Step Pyramid at Saqqara (above left). It had six 'steps', each one smaller than the one below it. It was the burial place of King Djoser in about 2611 BC. About 60 years later, the Egyptians learned how to build true pyramids by using packing blocks to fill in the 'steps'. Occasionally things went wrong. When the Bent Pyramid (above right) was half built, the architects decided to change the angle so that the top half is much more steeply inclined than the bottom.

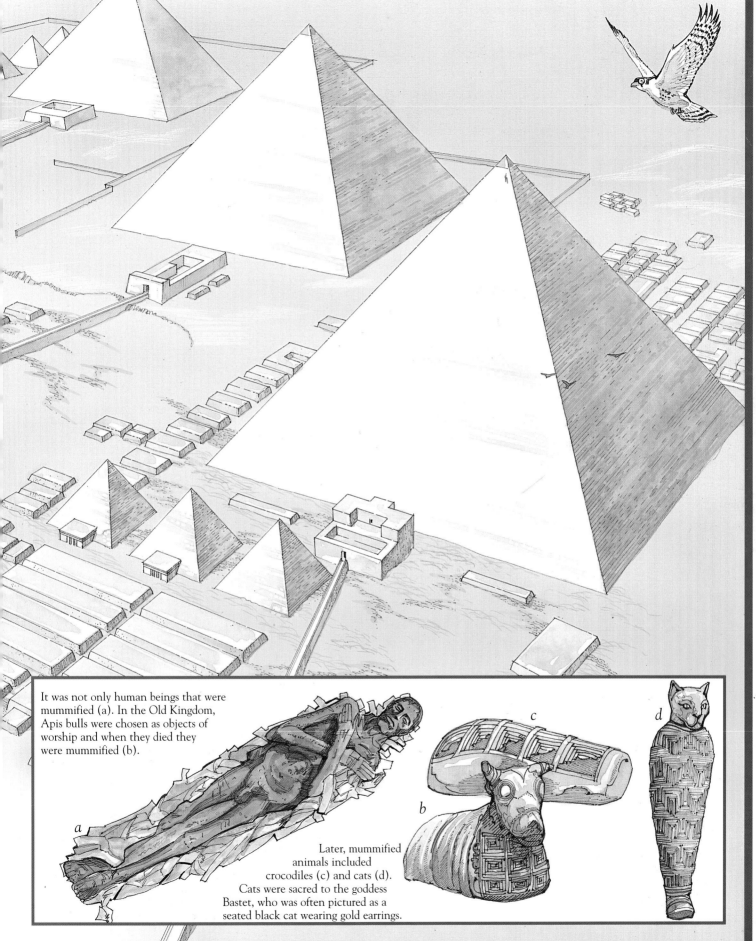

It was not only human beings that were mummified (a). In the Old Kingdom, Apis bulls were chosen as objects of worship and when they died they were mummified (b).

Later, mummified animals included crocodiles (c) and cats (d). Cats were sacred to the goddess Bastet, who was often pictured as a seated black cat wearing gold earrings.

Preparing the Mummy

Egypt is a very hot country, so when a person died his or her body was taken away at once to be mummified. It took 70 days to complete the whole process. First, the brain was removed through the nostrils with an iron hook. Then a cut was made in the abdomen through which all the internal organs were removed, including the lungs, stomach and intestines. The body was then thoroughly washed with palm wine followed by water mixed with ground spices. When it was as clean as possible, the inside was filled with sweet-smelling herbs and spices and the cut sewn up.

The body was dried out in a bath of natron, a form of salt. After 40 days the skin looked like leather. It was then oiled and stuffed where necessary to make it look lifelike and wrapped from head to foot in strips of linen bandages. Amulets were placed in particular positions inside the bandages, and finally a mask was put over the head.

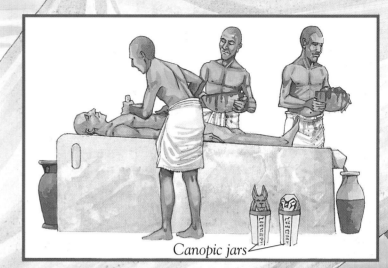

Canopic jars

The embalmers worked on the newly dead body, removing the internal organs (above). Sometimes these were thrown into the river or buried, but for more important mummies they were placed in special containers called canopic jars, which were buried with the mummy itself.

Natron bath

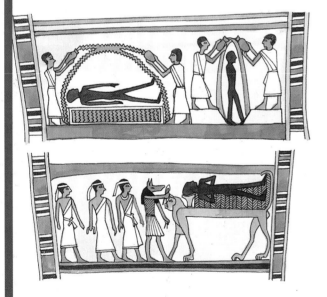

This copy of an ancient wall painting shows the priests washing the body and pouring water over the head (top). The body is then laid on a couch (bottom) while the priest, dressed as the jackal-headed god of the underworld, Anubis, reads out magic spells.

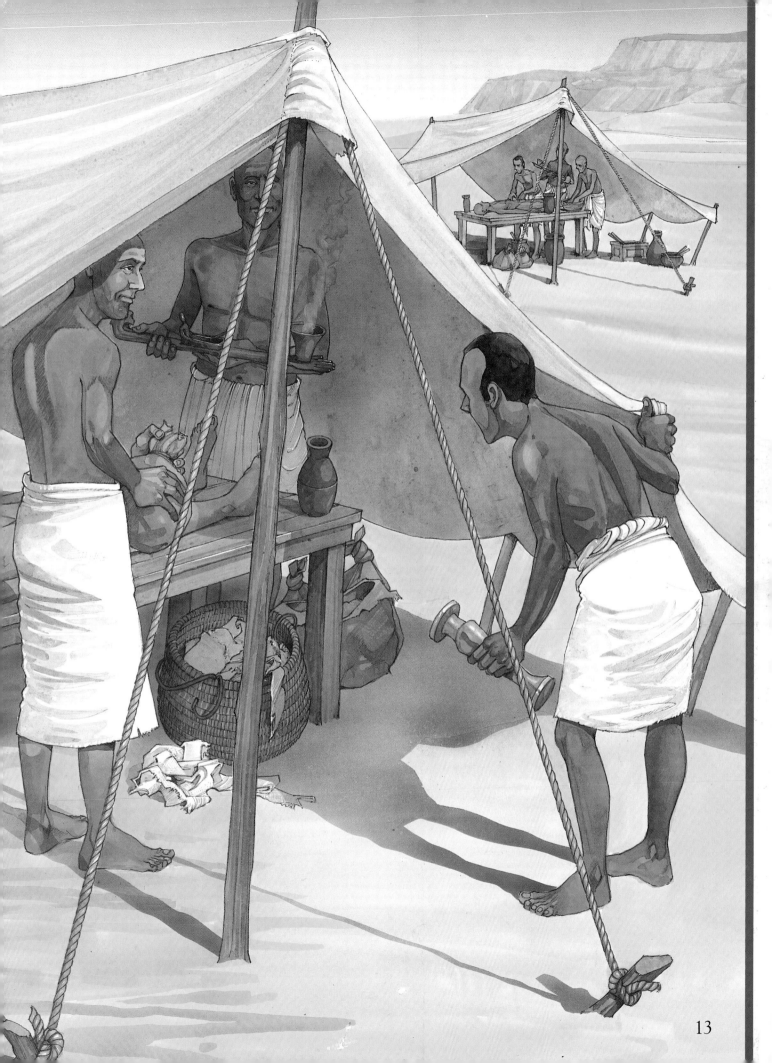

Wrapping the Mummy

Once the embalmers had done their work on the body, it was time for priests to wrap it in linen. Flax, from which linen is made, was grown throughout Egypt's history. However, linen was an expensive material and some mummies were wrapped in recycled linen strips. Quite often, garments the deceased had worn in life were torn up to provide their mummy wrappings. In later periods, special linen sheets were woven and then torn into strips.

As the wrapping process progressed, priests chanted spells. Some later mummies had spells written directly on to the wrappings themselves. Amulets were carefully inserted in specially designated places as protection devices and to ward off evil spirits.

For more elaborate mummies, the fingers and toes were individually wrapped. Egyptologists know from the mummy of King Tutankhamun that royal fingers and toes had special gold covers pushed over them. The covers, called finger or toe stalls, had the fingernails and toenails beautifully drawn on them. Tutankhamun's mummy also wore golden sandals with curled toes and a thong that ran between the big toe and the next.

Toe stall

Finger stall

Liquid resin

Linen for mummy wrapping

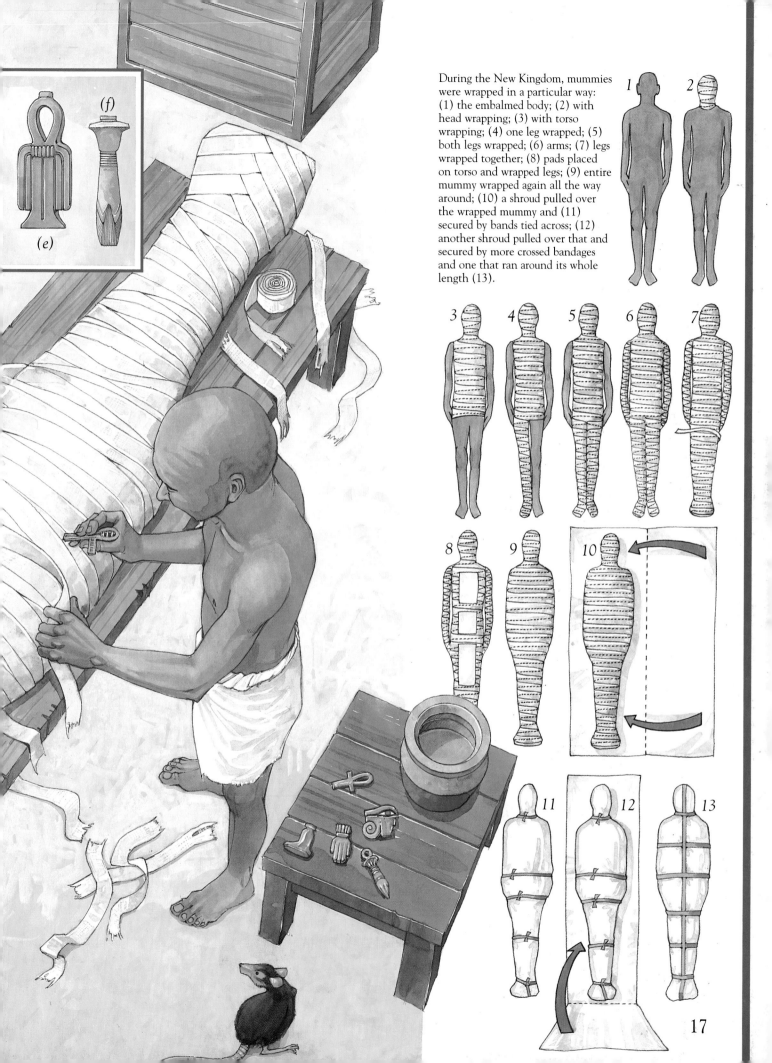

During the New Kingdom, mummies were wrapped in a particular way: (1) the embalmed body; (2) with head wrapping; (3) with torso wrapping; (4) one leg wrapped; (5) both legs wrapped; (6) arms; (7) legs wrapped together; (8) pads placed on torso and wrapped legs; (9) entire mummy wrapped again all the way around; (10) a shroud pulled over the wrapped mummy and (11) secured by bands tied across; (12) another shroud pulled over that and secured by more crossed bandages and one that ran around its whole length (13).

17

Mummy Cases and Coffins

In the Old Kingdom, coffins were usually rectangular wooden boxes with a single line of painted text asking for food in the afterlife. Sometimes they were painted with a pair of eyes so that the mummy could 'see' out.

Later coffins were more brightly painted, with spells on the inside and more decoration outside. Rectangular coffins were more or less abandoned in favour of anthropoid coffins – wooden boxes in the shape of a human body. These coffins could be very elaborate indeed and highly coloured. In simple burials, the mummy was placed in one anthropoid coffin within a large stone chest, called a sarcophagus. Royal burials involved a number of decorated anthropoid coffins, each fitting neatly into the next and all placed in a sarcophagus.

This golden mask of the boy king Tutankhamun (above) is thought to be an exact likeness of him. The mask was made from beaten gold, inlaid with precious stones and coloured glass paste. On his forehead, the king wore the uraeus, representing the dual land of Upper and Lower Egypt. This and the false beard beneath his chin are symbols of kingship.

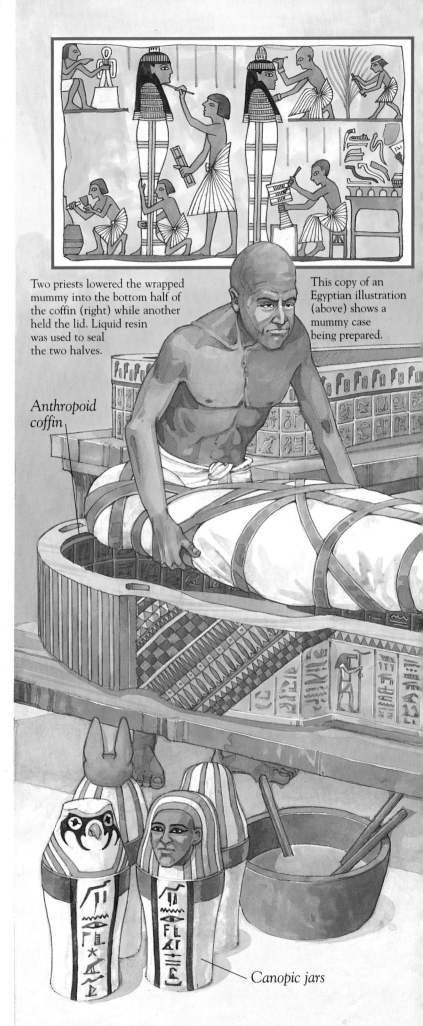

Two priests lowered the wrapped mummy into the bottom half of the coffin (right) while another held the lid. Liquid resin was used to seal the two halves.

This copy of an Egyptian illustration (above) shows a mummy case being prepared.

Anthropoid coffin

Canopic jars

18

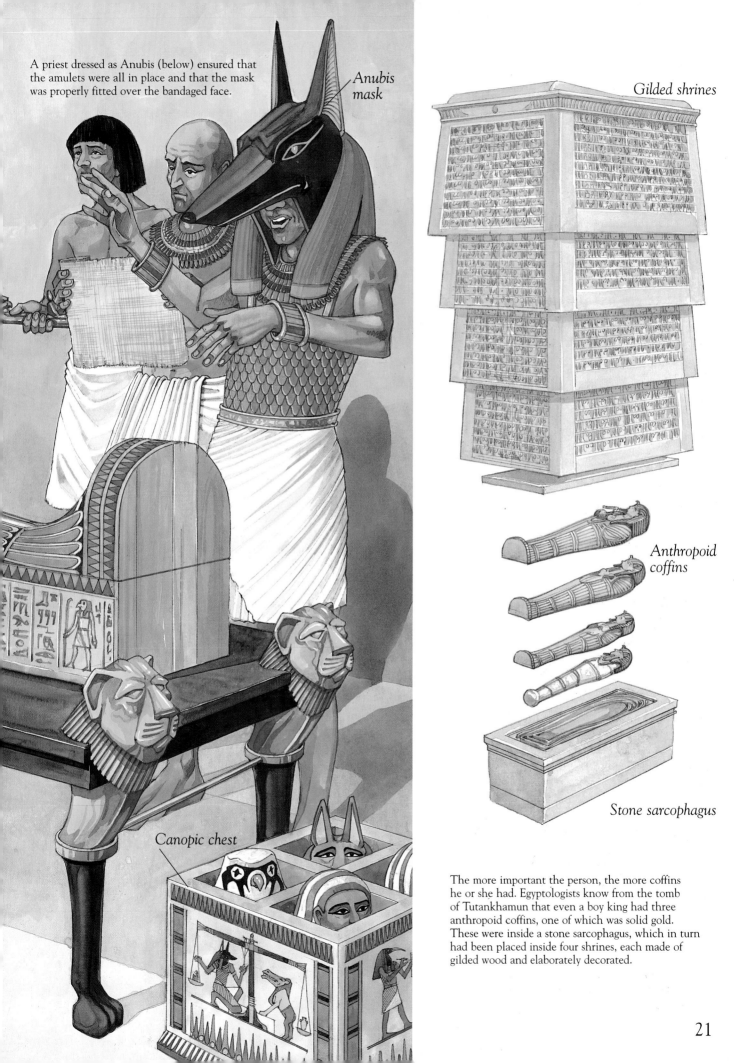

A priest dressed as Anubis (below) ensured that the amulets were all in place and that the mask was properly fitted over the bandaged face.

Anubis mask

Canopic chest

Gilded shrines

Anthropoid coffins

Stone sarcophagus

The more important the person, the more coffins he or she had. Egyptologists know from the tomb of Tutankhamun that even a boy king had three anthropoid coffins, one of which was solid gold. These were inside a stone sarcophagus, which in turn had been placed inside four shrines, each made of gilded wood and elaborately decorated.

21

The Funeral Procession

Once the mummy was placed in its coffin or coffins, it was ready to be transported to the place of burial, where the great stone sarcophagus was waiting. The tomb itself had to be ready and well prepared with everything the dead person might need in the afterlife: food and drink, clothes, furniture, jewels, chariots and even servants. The 'servants' were little pottery models called shabti figures, which the ancient Egyptians believed could stand in for the dead person's servants and do any hard work that might be required in the afterlife, such as cultivating crops for food. Some tombs contained hundreds of shabtis. They were usually glazed a brilliant blue and had a spell from the Book of the Dead inscribed on them so that they could answer the call to service.

The coffin was first placed in an open shrine on a papyrus boat (below). The boat was dragged on a sledge from the place of mummification to the dead person's home so that the family could accompany the deceased on his or her final journey. Then the boat was dragged down to the edge of the river. Burial sites were on the west bank of the Nile, as the west was considered sacred.

As the funeral procession approached the riverbank, more and more people would join it until quite a crowd had gathered. Friends and neighbours might carry some of the objects that were to stock the tomb (above).

Life expectancy was very short in ancient Egypt and most people died long before middle age. Burials were a part of everyday life, and in larger villages and towns there were professional mourners – usually women – who joined the funeral procession (above). They wore blue to show they were mourning.

As the boat was rowed across the river (above), the mourners sang and wailed. When it reached the other side, the shrine was taken off, placed on a sledge and dragged by oxen to the tomb. At the tomb the coffin was removed and placed upright against one of the walls inside. Priests then performed rituals in front of the coffin.

Funeral procession crosses to the west bank of the River Nile

Opening-of-the-Mouth Ceremony

The most important ritual was the opening-of-the-mouth ceremony (right). To enable the dead person to eat and drink in the underworld, his mouth had to be 'opened' by magic. It was also necessary to 'open' his nose so he could breathe, his ears so he could hear and his eyes so he could see. There were special instruments for doing this, usually types of flint knives, but sometimes the right leg bone of an ox was used. The ritual was usually performed by the eldest son and heir of the dead person.

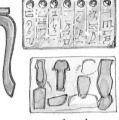

Instruments for the opening-of-the-mouth

Thoth

Anubis

Ammut

Ma'at

Feather of Truth

When the mummy reached the underworld, it had to undergo a final judgement before Osiris. The heart of the dead person was weighed against the feather of Ma'at, the goddess of truth (left). The dead person had to swear before 42 judges that he or she had done no wrong in life. Passing the test allowed them into the underworld and they were declared 'true of voice'.

Stocking the Tomb

Very few ancient Egyptian tombs have survived intact. The only royal tomb that lay undisturbed until modern times was that of King Tutankhamun. From this tomb Egyptologists have learned a great deal about the objects that were placed in a burial, especially a royal one.

After the exciting discovery of Tutankhamun's tomb in November 1922, Howard Carter and his team of experts found a vast horde of treasures. The tomb had four chambers, including the burial chamber itself, which contained the sarcophagus hidden inside four golden shrines. The other three rooms were full of the most extraordinary objects. In one chamber alone, they found 171 different items and pieces of furniture, including four chariots and a bronze trumpet.

The chief official directed the placing of the objects in the tomb. Boxes contained items such as jewels folded in rolls of linen, clothing, riding gloves and sandals. The boxes were wooden with flat lids, domed or made of reeds. Sometimes they had a list of their contents written in ink on the outside. There were stools, beds, chairs and jars made of pottery or alabaster. A huge black wooden statue of Anubis kept watch over the preparations.

Tomb robbery was considered such a terrible crime that those caught were sentenced to death.

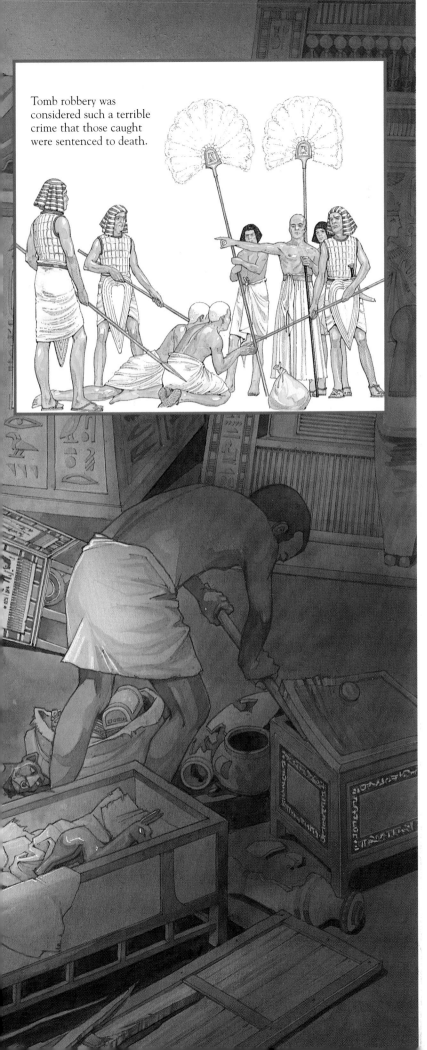

Shabtis were often placed all together in a special wooden chest (above). On the outside were recorded the name and titles of the dead person. It was thought that in the afterlife, the dead person only had to ask one of his shabtis to do a certain task and the shabti would reply, 'I am here'.

An offering table made of reeds held baskets of food (below). On the shelves were birds and the baskets in front held flat loaves of bread and cakes made with honey and dates. Egypt's hot, dry climate has meant that these objects have survived thousands of years, though they have become very dry.

Boats were occasionally placed in burials (below), in case the mummy had to travel across water in the underworld. They were usually left unfinished, to fit inside the tomb, but every part would be there, ready to be put together.

More Mummies

The ancient Egyptians were not the only people who mummified their dead, though they were the first and the most skilled. About AD 200-600, the Nazca people of Peru also mummified their dead. The soft tissue was removed and the body packed with cotton and lime. The tendons of the legs and arms were cut so that the body could be neatly curled up. It was then dried out above glowing coals before being wrapped in cloth and put in a funerary pot.

Other bodies have been mummified naturally. In 1991, the body of a man was discovered in ice in an alpine pass, where it had lain for nearly 5,000 years. It is thought that he was a traveller who had been overcome by hunger and exhaustion and died. In Greenland, on the edge of the Arctic Circle, the bodies of six women, one 4-year-old child and a baby were found in 1972. It was thought that the bodies had been mummified by the low temperatures and cold dry winds of the region.

An ill-fated Arctic expedition led by the British in the mid-nineteenth century ended in the entire team freezing to death. Their bodies were naturally mummified in the ice and snow.

This body of a young boy (right) was found buried in rocks. His head protruded from them and had decayed, but his body was naturally mummified in the dense soil that surrounded it. It is thought he was a human sacrifice to the gods of the Andes region of South America.

South American mummy

Inca mummy

This Inca boy (left) was probably another human sacrifice. His body was abandoned on a high mountain in the Andes and mummified naturally in the thin, cold air. He was curled up with his legs drawn up to his chest. His head, with its braided hair, rested on his folded arms.

Mummified baby found in Greenland

The group of mummies found in Greenland date to about AD 1475. The mummified baby (left) is thought to be about six months old. He was fully clothed in sealskin. The skin of his face, as well as his hair and eyebrows, were preserved. One of the female mummies in the same grave was probably his mother. This female mummy (right) was probably only about 30 years old when she died judging by her hands, which showed little sign of wear.

Mummified woman found in Greenland

The young man found in the alpine pass was well equipped for his journey (right). He had a deerskin quiver and arrows, a flint dagger and an axe. His clothes had been lined with straw to make them warm and windproof, and he had food and medicine with him. He probably died in about 3000 BC.

The alpine mummy had very well preserved hands.

The dense soil of peat bogs can naturally preserve bodies – it prevents oxygen from breaking down the organic matter in the body and makes the skin tough and leathery. Usually the face is preserved and looks very lifelike. Bodies can remain in peat bogs for 2,000 years or more, left undisturbed until peat cutters uncover them. Many hundreds of 'bog people' have been discovered in northwest Europe, and their bodies date to between 400 BC and AD 200. Most of these seem to have died violently, probably as sacrifices to gods.

This body of a girl (left), aged about 14, was found in a bog in Germany. It is thought that rather than being sacrificed to the gods, she had probably done something wrong, since her head had been partly shaved and she wore a blindfold (below). Her body had sunk into the bog after being weighed down with stones.

Lindow Man

This is the face of 'Lindow Man' (above left), named after the place in Cheshire where his body was discovered in 1984. He is shown as he looked when discovered, and on the right, a reconstruction shows how he probably looked in life, 2000 years ago. Wounds on his head showed he died a violent death.

'Tollund Man' (right) was discovered at the place of that name in Denmark. He had been hanged before his body was thrown into the bog as a sacrifice. He was naked and his only possessions were his cap and belt. Still knotted around his neck was the noose that had been used to hang him.

Tollund Man

Glossary

Afterlife
The place where dead Egyptians arrived after passing through the underworld.

Ammut
A creature of the underworld with the head of a crocodile, the chest and front legs of a lioness and the hindquarters of a hippopotamus.

Amulet
A small object like a lucky charm that was placed among the bandages of a mummy to ward off evil and keep the mummy safe on its way to the underworld.

Anthropoid coffins
Wooden boxes in the shape of a human body. They had two parts: the bottom half, in which the body was placed, and the lid, which was then sealed onto the base.

Anubis
The jackal-headed god of the underworld. The ancient Egyptians believed that he invented mummification.

Apis Bull
These were real bulls, chosen for their special markings (black and white with a diamond shape on their foreheads) that lived in palaces and were worshipped as gods. When an Apis bull died, he was mummified and buried in a special cemetery called the Serapeum.

Ba
The *ba* was believed to be the personality of a person. It was the duty of the *ba* to fly between the tomb and the underworld and to help the dead person reach the afterlife safely.

Book of the Dead
This was a series of spells, divided into 190 chapters. Some spells were recited during the mummification and funeral, while others were placed in the tomb to help the dead person in his or her journey to the afterlife.

Ka
The *ka* was a person's life force. When the person died, his *ka* lived on in his mummy.

Ma'at
The goddess of truth, justice and order.

Malachite
A bright green stone used in ancient Egyptian jewellery or ground into powder and used as eye make-up.

Natron
A form of natural salt used for drying out a body during the mummification process.

Offerings
Many tombs contained a representation of a table of offerings so that the *ka* would have food in the afterlife. It was usually shown piled high with fowl, bread, vegetables and fruit.

Old Kingdom, Middle Kingdom and New Kingdom
The three main periods of Egyptian history when the pharaoh and the state were in full control. The Old Kingdom lasted from 2686-2181 BC and is also known as the Pyramid Age. Then came the First Intermediate Period (2181-2055 BC) – a time of unhappiness and chaos. The Middle Kingdom (2055-1650 BC) saw Egypt reunited into one country again and art and literature flourished. The Second Intermediate Period (1650-1550 BC) was another time of disorder, when a foreign race called the Hyksos took over the north of the country. Egypt was reunited for the glorious period of the New Kingdom (1550-1069 BC) when it was the supreme world power.

Osiris
The god of the dead. He was murdered by his brother Seth and Anubis made him into the first mummy. He is often symbolised by

a djed-pillar, probably meant to represent his backbone.

Pottery plaque
A piece of baked clay painted to represent an eye and placed over the eye sockets of a mummy.

Professional mourners
These were usually women, hired to join an Egyptian funeral procession. They made a great deal of noise, loudly lamenting and wailing. They also threw their heads back and made a gargling sound. This was called ululation and still occurs in Egypt today.

Resin
The sweet-smelling sap that oozes from fir and pine trees.

Sarcophagus (pl. Sarcophagii)
A large outer coffin, usually made of stone.

Shabtis
Pottery (and occasionally wood or stone) figurines in human shape buried with a mummy. Shabtis were called upon to do manual labour in the underworld for the dead person. Tutankhamun was buried with over 400 shabtis.

Thoth
The god of wisdom and writing. Sometimes he is shown as an ibis, sometimes as a baboon. He kept a record of how long a person was to live and what would happen to them.

Tyet-knot
A symbol sacred to the goddess Isis, representing a sandal strap.

Uraeus
A symbol worn on the forehead by the Egyptian king, both in life and death. It usually consisted of a cobra and a vulture and symbolised the power of the two goddesses who guarded Lower and Upper Egypt, Wadjyt and Nehkbet.

Mummies Facts

Tutankhamun was a boy king in the late New Kingdom. Egyptologists would know very little about him had it not been for the discovery of his nearly intact tomb by Howard Carter in 1922. Because his tomb contained such marvellous treasures, he became renowned throughout the world. During the 1920s and 1930s, there was a craze called Tutmania, which produced all sorts of things inspired by the discovery, for example sewing machines, cigarettes, dances and music.

In the months that followed the discovery of Tutankhamun's tomb in 1922, various people connected with the discovery died unusual deaths. Lord Carnarvon, who had paid for the search for the tomb, died suddenly of blood poisoning after being bitten on the cheek by a mosquito. Two others died: one was run over crossing the road and another fell out of a window. This gave rise to a belief in the 'Curse of the Mummy'. Egyptologists do not take the curse seriously, but it has been the source of much amusement and debate.

Spells that were painted on the inside of coffins are referred to as Coffin Texts by Egyptologists. They were there to help the dead person avoid danger and arrive safely in the afterlife.

The ancient Egyptian symbol for a person's *ba* was a bird with a human head and arms. The *ka* was shown as a pair of upraised arms.

During the 16th and 17th centuries AD, ground mummy powder was considered a powerful drug and people swallowed it for medicinal purposes. The ills it was supposed to cure ranged from sore throats and coughs to epilepsy and tuberculosis. Other people believed that if mummy powder was applied to a wound, the bleeding would stop. Because mummy powder was believed to be so powerful, many thousands of Egyptian mummies were broken up and ground down.

In Walt Disney's animated film *Snow White and the Seven Dwarfs*, mummy powder is used by the wicked stepmother in one of her evil spells.

There was a paint called Mummy Brown used in the 19th century for oil painting. This was actually made from little bits of mummies. One artist who discovered this was so horrified that he took his tubes of Mummy Brown out into the garden and gave them a proper burial! There is still a colour called mummy brown.

The ancient Egyptians called the huge area of barren land in their country *deshret*, meaning red land. This is the source of our word 'desert'.

Over a period of 3,000 years, the exact way in which an ancient Egyptian mummy was bandaged changed. Sometimes the linen strips were wide, sometimes narrow. One woman was found wrapped in 16 layers of bandages, and a man mummified during the Middle Kingdom was wrapped in no less than 375 square metres of linen.

Some ancient Egyptians grew so fond of their pets that when the animals died, they had them mummified and asked that they be placed in their tombs when they themselves died. Mummified gazelles, monkeys, dogs and baboons have been found in tombs.

One tomb owner was so fond of his pet dog that he asked for its linen-wrapped mummy to be put at his feet in his coffin.

All mummies had their hearts weighed against the feather of truth before they could enter the underworld. This ritual is described in Chapter 125 of the Book of the Dead and was often illustrated on papyrus scrolls buried with the dead person. There is no record of anyone failing the test, but the underworld demon Ammut was sometimes shown waiting by the weighing scales to devour the heart of anyone whose evil deeds betrayed them. Without a heart, the dead person could not survive in the afterlife.

Thousands of sacred cats inhabited temples dedicated to the Egyptian cat goddess Bastet. They were mummified and buried when they died and a huge number of cat mummies remain to this day.

Masks have always played an important part in the decoration of mummies. The earliest mummy masks found in Peru date to around 1200 BC and were made of red or brown cloth, which was stitched to the mummy dressing. In later periods burial masks were made of hammered sheet gold or copper with separate noses and teeth soldered on.

The ancient Incas mummified bodies by first filling them with tar and then exposing them alternately to severe frost at night and to the heat of the sun by day, until they were dried out completely. Then the body was placed in a niche or cave, where it did not rest undisturbed, but was frequently taken out for festivities such as the celebration of military victories. The mummy would be taken to the place of celebration, dressed in sumptuous garments, seated on a golden chair and given food and drink while people danced before it.

Index

Illustrations are shown in **bold** type.

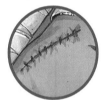